Waves of Grace

Written By:

Patrick James Norman

Dedication

To my dear friend and her beautiful family— Who followed the call of the sea and the whisper of grace, Who traded comfort for courage and found something eternal in the rhythm of the waves.

Your move to the beach was more than a relocation—it was a transformation. In the crashing surf and quiet sunrises, you found faith. In the simple joys and challenges of starting anew, you became a light for others, including me. Your journey is a testament to what happens when hearts open and God steps in.

Thank you for inspiring strength through surrender, joy through simplicity, and hope through devotion. Your story is woven into these pages with love, wonder, and gratitude.

Introduction

When she moved to the coast, it was meant to be practical—a quieter life, a softer rhythm. But the waves had other plans. This is the story of a family whose journey became a testimony, where sunrises invited reflection and laughter echoed like worship. From the hush of morning coffee by the pool to the shoreline prayers spoken beneath stars, each page holds a whisper of grace and a footprint of love. Anchored by faith, inspired by everyday miracles, and knit together through tender rituals, their story invites us to see holiness in the ordinary and hope in the breeze. This story is told by her herself.

When we moved to the coast, I thought it would be a practical shift—better hours, slower living. But the peace I found wasn't just in the warm air or gentle surf.

It was in Jesus quietly meeting me in every moment. Our house became more than a home—it became our sanctuary.

Most mornings, I sat quietly beside our pool, coffee warming my hands before the sun fully woke. That moment—before the world began asking anything of me—was sacred. I'd watch the shimmer of light across the water, feeling the hush of grace settle deep. My husband's quiet strength lingered in my mind, like the still ripples on the surface, steady and true. With each sip, I felt Jesus near—gentle, grounding me before the day began.

4

My grandson came to see me most weekends, running ahead in search of shells on the beach. His joy was radiant. I saw God's work in him, in the care of my daughter who is a new mother, and in the quiet patterns our family had begun to shape.

6

One afternoon, we all sat near the shore—my husband, our son recently married, our grandson nestled beside me. The tide rolled in gently, silencing every worry. In that stillness, I felt the echo of grace, wrapped in laughter and love.

My husband bent down, picked up a smooth stone, and handed it to our grandson. "Life shapes us," he told him. "And it strengthens us too." I watched the boy turn that stone, absorbing something deep beyond words.

10

A crab scurried across our path, and I couldn't help but laugh. "God leads us in odd ways sometimes," I told our son. "Even when the path doesn't make sense to us." He smiled, the truth of those words echoing in the songs he plays at church and the new love he had found here.

12

We lay back in the sand and stared into the sky. I thought of our oldest daughter, living farther away.

Even separated by miles, she was still under that same sky—still held, still loved.

14

Before we went home my grandson asked why seagulls aren't afraid. My husband answered simply, "They know who holds the wind." And in that moment, I felt that reassurance settle over all of us—we are held too, even when we can't see it.

One Sunday, we stepped into a new church close to the beach. The atmosphere clicked— warm smiles, amazing worship, and the truth was there. My husband leaned close and whispered that he felt God here. The next week we made it our Church home.

My husband and our son joined the worship team. They carved out time between work and rehearsals.

I watched our grandson tap along beside me, learning that praise is something we pass down, not just perform.

I've come to believe love doesn't always crash in—it flows. In our marriage, motherhood, and even in long-distance longing, love reshapes life just like the tide reshapes the shore. This reshaping can bring us closer together even though we are far apart.

After services, we'd walk along the shoreline. Sometimes we shared thoughts.

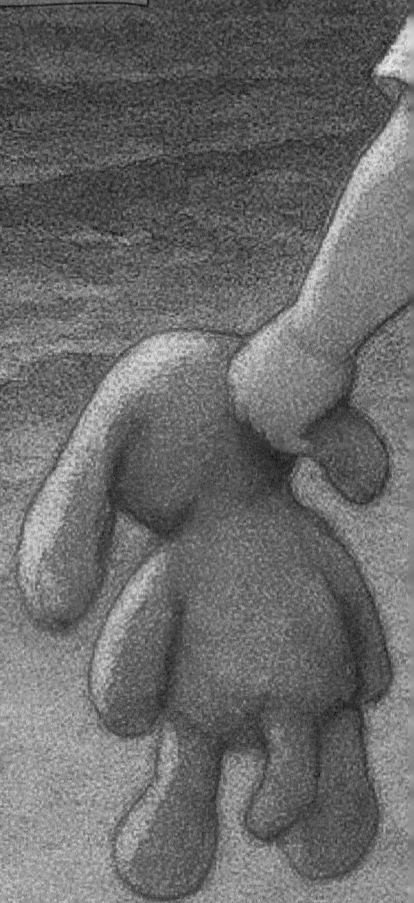

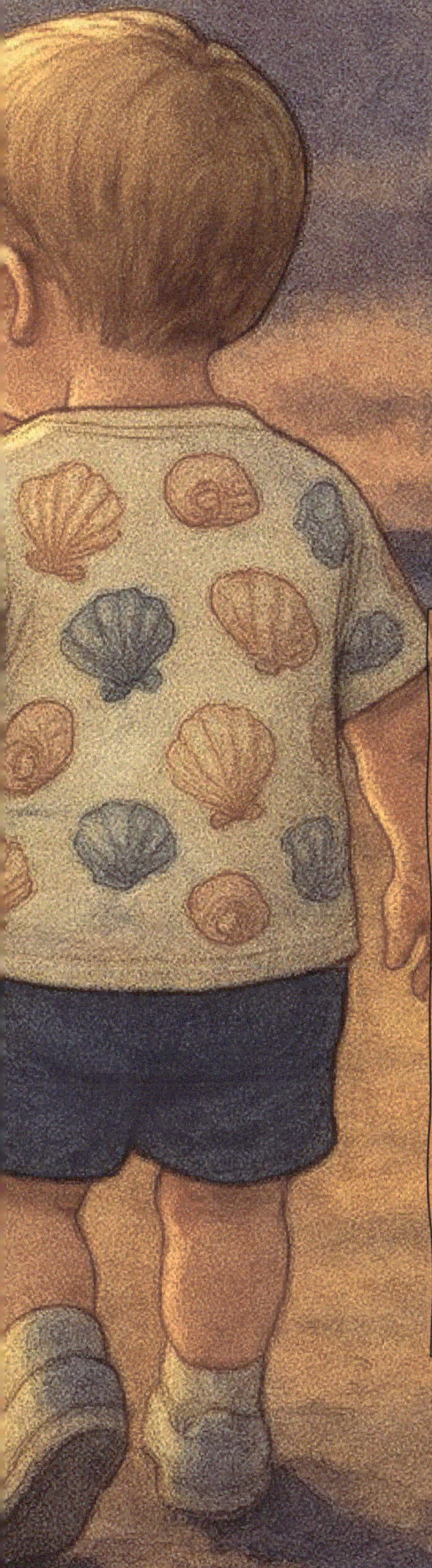

Sometimes we walked in silence. But always, I sent my prayers into the wind—especially for my kids and grandson.

25

We stayed to watch the sunset, glowing gold against the waves. My grandson gasped when the clouds lit like embers. We didn't speak. We just stood together, grateful for a love that warms even the edges of our lives.

As stars appeared one by one, my grandson lay beside me on a blanket. I whispered, "Even in the dark, the light hasn't left." I pray he carries those words with him always.

29

That night, as we finished our prayers, I looked over at my grandson—the waves behind him, faith before him, love surrounding us both. It felt whole. Sacred.

BIBLE

Each morning, my husband rose before anyone else—just to make coffee the way I love it. I watched him, Bible open, bathed in sunlight on the porch. His quiet consistency became a devotion all its own.

Our daughter, who is a new mother, visits often. We talk about motherhood, faith, and the way women carry joy and responsibility at once. She asks deep questions, and I cherish the wisdom blooming between us.

My oldest daughter lives further away. Our phone calls fill the gap, stitched together by prayer and love. I often whisper this prayer, "Protect her. Keep her close."

My husband taught our grandson how to fish—not just with rod and reel, but with patience and storytelling.

The boy listened closely, absorbing memories with every cast.

One day, after we built sandcastles, all of us. My grandson laughed when they fell. "That's okay," I said. "God doesn't promise permanence—only love." And just like that, we began building again.

40

41

Rain once interrupted a picnic. We hid under a quilt, telling stories and sipping hot tea. My husband winked and said, "Even storms rinse the soul." I knew exactly what he meant.

One afternoon, my grandson sat drawing—shells, waves, a smiling sky. "It's our beach," he said. In his colored pencil strokes, I saw the fingerprints of God.

43

44

My oldest daughter who lives away surprised us with a visit. The moment I saw her, tears welled. My husband placed his hands on her shoulders and prayed—not just for reunion, but for courage and protection.

We gathered around the firepit that evening. Our son played guitar, his wife hummed, and my husband slipped a marshmallow into our grandson's hand like a treasure.

The sweetness lingered, but it was love that nourished us.

Through all this experience I found that our Grandson was a new light within us. You never really know how much you can love someone until you get married and have kids of your own, but having a grandson seemed to bring all of us even closer together.

One day my grandson asked if Jesus lived in the ocean. I knelt beside him. "He lives in everything," I said.

"In your laugh. In Papa's care. In Mama's hugs." He smiled, and I knew that truth had settled deeply.

Someone from church told me our family radiates peace and love. I smiled. Peace isn't the absence of struggle—it's the anchor we cling to.

And that anchor has always
been Jesus.

One afternoon, my husband surprised me with a custom chair set for our pool area with our wedding date underneath. "For sitting together," he said. I cried—not because of the years behind us, but for every moment ahead.

Another day we all walked the beach together—our footprints trailing behind us. My grandson chased gulls with his net laughing, my oldest daughter laughed with her father, and our son held his wife's hand. I lingered at the back, heart overflowing.

As the sun sank, we gathered in a circle. My husband prayed aloud. Then we sang—not perfectly, but joyfully.

That shoreline became our holy ground—where love had grown, where grace had met us, again.

THE END

64

65

• STOP PUTTING PRESSURE ON YOURSELF
THAT GOD ISN'T PUTTING ON YOU.
YOU CAN TURN A DEFEAT INTO
A STRENGTH.

ANCHOR YOUR ✝
IDENTITY IN WHAT
CAN'T BE TAKEN
AWAY.

THE TRUE
TREASURE IS
JESUS.

OUR IDENTITY IS IN CHRIST.
OUR CITIZENSHIP IS IN HEAVEN.
DENY YOURSELF AND PICK UP YOUR
CROSS.
YOU CAN GAIN THE WHOLE WORLD

66

"If I take the wings of the morning, And dwell in the uttermost parts of the sea; Even there shall thy hand lead me, And thy right hand shall hold me." —*Psalm 139:9–10 (ASV)*

www.ingramcontent.com/pod-product-compliance
Lightning Source LLC
Chambersburg PA
CBHW040317100426
42811CB00012B/1467